GET RICH FOR BEGINNERS

I WILL HELP BEGINNERS REACH THEIR FINANCIAL GOALS IN A NUTSHELL

Contents

WHY NOT BE RICH?

Many people find it hard to make money because many people seek the fast and easy way to make money. You see, many people end up making the wrong decisions about why they go into the company, and some people think it's an instant overnight thing to create wealth. There's so much hype about it, I think, that you take a look at newspaper ads, and it claims some stuff about total earnings, and so on.

And one thing that is important in creating wealth and, particularly, in learning about business or investment is that you must read it and digest it quickly. It's time and initiative you should be prepared to invest. People don't make money easily because, in terms of the mindset of wealth, many of us have been brainwashed by the media, so to speak, we have the wrong wealth concept.

An example here. What makes a person wealthy, if I ask people?

People say that's how much you earn, the car you drive, and your own house. It isn't true. It's not how much you earn because there are people I know who earn 20,000 dollars a month, which are broken. And some people make $3,000 a month who are wealthy because they're all spending it. Many people know that I have to buy a bigger home and a bigger car to be rich by watching many films and looking at the media.

So, in the end, all their money is spent, all their time buying what they call negative cash flow assets, making them poorer and poorer. And they are not investing in cash flow assets that are positive. And even if they do, they do it in such a way that they lose everything because they don't understand what they're doing, similar to a stock market casino idea. So, this is the main reason they're losing money. They're not able to be rich.

Here are what I think are the reasons people don't get rich.

Who Are My?

The first is that it never happens to them at the top of the list.

The average individual grew up in a family where he never met or knew someone rich. He goes to school and socializes with individuals who are not affluent. He works with individuals who are not wealthy. Outside of work, he has a reference group or a social circle who are not wealthy. He doesn't have wealthy role models. You may grow up and be a fully-refined adult in our society if this happens to you during your formation years up to the age of twenty. It can never happen to you that you will be as wealthy as anybody else as possible.

It is why it is much more likely that people who grow up in homes where their parents are wealthy will become wealthy as adults than people who have grown up in homes where their parents are not.

So the first reason people don't become wealthy is that it never happens to them that they can do it. And naturally, they never take steps to make it a reality if it never happens to them.

Make A Decision

The second reason people don't become wealthy is that they never choose to do so.

Although someone is reading a book, taking part in a lecture, or working with financially successful people, Nothing changes until they decide to do something else. Even if it happens to a person that he could become wealthy if he just did certain things in a particular way, he ends up staying as he is if he does not decide to take the first step.

If you keep doing what you have always done, you will continue to get what you always have.

The primary reason for failure and failure is that most individuals do not choose to succeed. They never make a firm, unambiguous dedication or decision that they will become wealthy. Someday, they mean to, and they intend to, and they hope to, and they will. "They wish and hope and pray that a lot of money will make, but they never decide, "I'm going to do it! This decision is a key first step towards financial independence.

Maybe Tomorrow

Procrastination is the third reason that people don't become wealthy.

To achieve financial independence, people always have a good reason not to begin doing what they know they need to do. The month is always wrong, the season is wrong, or the year is wrong. In their industry, business conditions aren't good, or they may be too good. The market's not right. They may be forced to take a risk or give up their safety. Next year maybe.

A reason to procrastinate always seems to be there. As a result, until it's too late, keep putting it off, month by month, year by year. Even if a person can become rich and has decided to change, a delay will lead all of his plans into the indefinite future.

Pay The Price

The fourth reason why poor people retire is what economists call the inability to delay gratification.

There is an irresistible temptation for most people to spend every single penny they make and whatever else they can borrow or purchase on credit. You can not become rich if you can not delay gratification, and discipline yourself to refrain from spending everything you make. It is impossible to achieve financial independence if you cannot practice budgeting as a lifelong custom.

As W.Clement Stone said, "The seeds of greatness are not in you if you can not save money."

Take The Long View

The fifth reason for the poor's retirement is perhaps as important, if not more important, than the rest...

It's a lack of perspective on time.

In a longitudinal study conducted at Harvard University by Dr. Edward Banfield in the 1950s and published as The Unheavenly City in 1964, he studied the reasons for upward socio-economic mobility. He wanted to understand how you could predict whether one or more socio-economic groups would move upwards and be wealthier in the next generation than they were in this generation.

All his research led him to a single factor that he concluded was more precise in predicting success in America than any other. They called it the perspective of time. It has been described as the amount of time you take into account when planning your daily activities and making important decisions in your life. The perspective of time referred to how far you projected into the future when you decided what in the present you were going to do or not.

An example of a long-term perspective is the common practice of higher-class English families. However, they will not visit Oxford or Cambridge for 18 or 19 years to register their children in England as soon as they are born. It is the perspective for a long time in action. The young couple who start to spend $50 a month on a scholarship fund to allow their newborn child to attend school or university is a long-term partner. To ensure better outcomes and results in the long term, they are willing to sacrifice in the short term. In the course of their lifetimes, people with a long time perspective almost invariably move up financially.

I know that it's never quick, quick, and easy to make real, good money. Even though I made my first $26 million, it didn't take me two years. It has taken more than that. A lot of hard work was needed. And most people think it's quick and easy, which is why it never leads to money.

IS THERE A REASON YOU WANT TO BE RICH?

I want to be rich. I said it there. Considered that I was a youngster, I frequently understood that I would be rich someday, and likewise, I have been significantly moving in that direction thinking about that. I made many mistakes, got to know myself a lot, and spent a lot of time considering why I want to be rich. I have been thinking, particularly for a long time, that my faith (I am a Christian) is rich and that I am a good steward of what I am entrusted with.

I thought about this issue, so I thought I'd share the reasons I want to be rich:

Encourage worthy causes

The means I see it, the more I have, the much more I can give away. In today's world, there are so many organizations and efforts that need money, and I'm excited to have the chance to contribute. I suppose many of these are more specific examples when I analyze the other items on this list.

Give great opportunities to my children.

I was blessed with two marvelous relatives who taught me all I need to know about life's most important things: faith, family, marriage, integrity, etc. I'm not from a rich family, however. My parents are smart people, but they didn't have the opportunity to go to college, nor did they have the resources to pay for my college trip. I have had the option to go to a fair school through the Navy, yet on occasion, I can't help thinking about what might have happened contrastingly had I left secondary school at MIT or Stanford instead of entering the Navy. I'd have had difficulty paying for it, and that is perhaps part of why I didn't see those schools as options. Without finances being what holds them back, I want my kids to have great opportunities. I want to help them pay for school, buy a house, start a company, etc. There's no guarantee they're going to succeed later on, but the least I can do is help them take the first step.

Give a chance to the underdog.

Here in San Francisco, one of my friends just got a job with a company and blogging his values as a company. "Helping outsiders and underdogs win" is one of them, and I can't stress enough how much I believe in this. I observed in recent years that the maxim, at least here out, is true "it's not what you know, it's who you know." I am extremely grateful that someone at CNET saw my Craigslist resume and sent me an e-mail to offer me a job as a product manager. I was just out of college, had no experience whatsoever, no connections, Nothing. They took me an opportunity, and I hope they'd say it's a good choice. Money opens doors, and I hope that I will have to use any influence to open the door to others who may not have the correct background. Somebody gave me a chance, and it made all the difference.

My Time's Own

Time is the most useful resource that many of us have. We get just so much of it (and we don't even know how much), and you can only do so to maximize the amount. You are unlikely to live much longer than a century, at least under current life expectancy, even if you eat healthily, exercise, be cautious, etc. (this could change, though). The point is, I hate my time being sold. I hate that I need things in life, and the only way I can get them is to sell my time in exchange for money. Granted, since I began freelancing, I've been selling my time for a lot more. And I've read about people who sell hundreds or thousands of dollars per hour of their time. But that's still slavery in my mind. It is a much more palatable form of slavery, but it is nevertheless slavery.

My objective is to reach a point where, through passive income sources, I can live a comfortable life. Unless I want to, I'll never have to get a job, pick up a client, or borrow money. I can spend my time pursuing the stuff that matters to me in life. And as a side note, I am not fully certain that the kind of financial security that money can buy cannot be regarded as happiness. With me, John agrees.

Explore the globe

Do you know this saying about how you end up owning the things you own? Well, that is true. If you want evidence, try to move frequently, ideally into smaller and smaller places slowly, so you have to get rid of things. It's so liberating to get rid of the junk you no longer need or even want. When we moved to San Francisco, my wife and I sold both our cars, and I'm so glad. Is it sometimes a pain? Yes. Yes. But just the peace of mind of not having to worry about a car is amazing, aside from the financial benefits (which are enormous).

I say all this to say that experiences are what I've come to value more than things. Things don't make you happy. My wife and I were blessed to walk around Asia for eleven weeks earlier this year, which was one of my most incredible experiences. I believe travel is one thing that, the more you do it, fundamentally shifts your perception of the world. I want the chance to live in some of the greatest cities in the world, to explore the cultures of the world, and to broaden my horizons by getting out and seeing how the other six billion people live.

Create riches for others

I saw Paul Graham, a renowned angel investor who has funded dozens (or cent) of startups, mainly in technology spaces, read this fantastic essay about riches one day. He talks in the essay about how many people see the world's wealth as fixed, and they, therefore, they see wealthy people as having taken more than their fair share. But in a zero-sum world, entrepreneurs do not work. Entrepreneurs generate wealth, and when they do, many other individuals get wealthy along the way, from investors to employees and even customers. Consider how much richer our lives are because of Gates' work, Steve Jobs, and the guys in Google. It rewarded them with billions for their work, but they also gave the world a great deal of wealth, both in monetary and technological progress.

For others, I want to create wealth and help make their dreams come true.

Change the globe

It brings me to the following point: entrepreneurs are transforming the world. In countless ways, the innovations they create make our lives richer. I believe that will foster so much innovation in the next few decades that the last few centuries will pale in comparison. In particular, I believe that advances in artificial intelligence/robotics, genetics, and nanotechnology will alter the world's face beyond recognition. I want to be part of these paradigm shifts, and wealth will allow me to fund great startups and start my businesses in these and other spaces.

Master myself

Finally, as I've heard, one of the best things about getting rich is not the destination but the journey. Becoming a millionaire is technically possible for most people, but statistically, few of them will. That's just too difficult. Controlling your finances, investing, starting a business, and other paths to wealth are all difficult for most people and require a lot of personal growth and development. One of John's best blog post lessons is the first: "I can get rich." It's much easier to do it again once you've done it because you believe in yourself and because, at least to some degree, you've mastered yourself.

I'm not waiting to do any of these things until I am "rich." I think wealth building is a process. There are no shortcuts on their own, but it is always possible to do it faster and smarter, but more risk, commitment, and time are necessary. No matter how I get there, I hope to keep these things in view and be good stewards of what I've been blessed with if and when I do. I want your remarks on the topic to be heard.

THE MENTALITY OF RICH

Have you ever heard people make comments about how that guy is "lucky" or "greedy" when they see a nice car-go by? Well, if you haven't, I know that if you wanted to, you could hear it very easily on a common street corner near your home. I think it's funny how people are willing to associate someone's wealth with greed and luck so quickly. Those people who think these things about wealthy people will never be so wealthy. If someone associates negative characteristics with becoming wealthy, then that's how they think they will achieve wealth. It takes someone to become wealthy to think like a millionaire, not like a pessimist.

How many individuals like to associate wealth with bad things is truly amazing. I used to think that rich people have long been bad people, too. To get what they had, I used to think they cheated, lied, and stole from other people. While reading a book about the mentality of rich people, I came to the point of realization. I realized that if I think of rich people that way, then first: I'll never want to be one subconsciously, and second: I'm associating the same bad thoughts with money itself. Let's say that I had to think the same way about an actual person in my life for some pretentious reason. At this point, that individual wouldn't have any desire to associate with me, I'm certain. Money operates in the same way. If you think money is all just a reward for lying, cheating, and stealing, then you are unbelievably doomed if you ever want to have any. Lying, cheating, and stealing are all going to land you in jail or dead before you ever get rich from them. The true path to wealth creation is hard work, faithful business behavior, and maximizing opportunities. They think of money as an old friend that they never get tired of seeing. Wealthy people don't associate money with bad things. The rich people believe that money is something they get through all their hard work. How are you referring to money?

Mindset Differences Between Rich People and Broken People

It's more profitable to leverage your strengths as a general rule than it is to fix your weaknesses.

It is particularly true when we're talking about abilities: concentrate on what you do well, and let someone else do the things you're struggling with.

However, there's one enormous exception to this general rule: bad mindsets.

A bad attitude isn't just an ordinary weakness but a critical weakness that will hamper your efficiency unless you address it.

The scarcity mindset is one example of an unhealthy mindset. The mentality of lack looks like wealth, success, and fame like a cake shot. There's so much to do, and everyone else gets less if one person takes too much of a slice.

Bill Gates is inherently evil in this worldview, no matter how much good he has done for society, notwithstanding how much he has helped others through his products and foundations. He's evil because he took a slice that was too big and didn't leave enough for the rest of us.

You have a scarcity mindset to the extent that you find yourself resenting rich and successful individuals.

It is difficult for you to be truly happy for others' success; you have a scarcity of thoughts.

The alternative to a scarcity mindset is a mindset of abundance. The mindset of abundance says that we can create more value for all. We can create win-win situations where everyone is better than before instead of looking at wealth and success as a zero-sum game.

You find it difficult to cooperate with others if you have little thought because your losses are their gains. If you have an attitude of bounty, you will work together effectively with others to make more esteem along these lines.

The phrase "creating value" is crucial to the mindset of abundance. Value, and therefore wealth, not only exists, it can be created. We're not limited to splitting the pie we have at the moment. We could make that pie bigger. New pies, we can make them.

If you want to move forward, you don't just want to look for your interests, and you want to look for others.

The best approach is to be generous instead of hosting suspiciously all you have to do until you see an opportunity to make it a profit. Generous of your time, generous of your knowledge, generous of your abilities.

If you think hard about exactly how it is done by the people who make a full-time living online, the easiest answer is generosity. They spend their time and energy creating valuable content that helps people and building a following of real fans, people who trust them and are grateful for their contributions. They have legions of eager clients when they finally release a product.

I once heard Darren Rowse describing his first product, the Digital Photography School and ProBlogger blogger. It was also an ebook called "31 Days to Build a Better Blog." He had several things recently and repackaged it as an eBook in an arrangement on his blog called "31 different ways to build a better blog."

Why would somebody want to purchase something free of charge online? One reason could be that you value the efficiency of having everything in one location, so you don't have to search his archives when you need the information. One explanation could be that people just like the idea of owning something.

However, several people who e-mailed him said they knew that the information was available free of charge, but they still purchased the ebook because it was the first occasion Darren had to thank for all he'd done for them.

For a second, think that his product offered little new value, but customers were happy to purchase it because Darren had created such an extra value for them.

Counter-intuitively is to give generously, one of the best strategies for getting ahead.

"The scarcity mindset must always ask, "What am I getting from this transaction?" "The spirit of abundance is free to ask, "What can I give in" this transaction?"

A book I read recently called Millionaire Mind Secrets by T is really interesting. Eker Harv. This book closely links you to your ability to become rich. The idea is to drive your thoughts and feelings and to determine the results of your actions.

He says people have "a thermostat of finance." Every individual is scheduled for a certain level of wealth, just as a house has a certain temperature. Just as the house's temperature can fluctuate even if the thermostat is on (the temperature outside the house could change quickly, or somebody might leave a window open), however, as long as the thermostat is on a certain level, it will default in the long term.

In his view, the only way to become truly rich is to reprogram the person's to alter your mindset related to money.

You need to dismiss the ways of thinking that hold you back and embrace thinking to advance you.

Here are "Wealth Files" that set out differences between how money is approached by the rich and the poor, as well as my commentary:

1) Rich people believe that "I create my life." Poor people think that "Life is happening to me."

Do you think that you can control the direction in which your life goes?

I hope most of you will say that you do, but do it back for you up with your actions?

You will take action to get where you want to go if you believe that you can control your life's direction. You won't if you don't. You're going to believe, instead, that you're just a victim of your circumstances.

It is easier to believe that because it lets you off the hook, life happens to you. That you're poor is not your fault for being overweight. Or incapable of finding a good spouse. All of these have been the result of the bad breaks that have come your way. All you're playing is the hand you've been dealt.

The reality is that everybody's going to have their fair share of bad breaks, but if you're proactively in control of your life instead of responding reactively, you're not broken by the bad breaks.

In any self-improvement journey, the first step is to admit that you can and are responsible for making things better.

2) The money game to win is played by rich people. Poor people play the game of money in order not to lose.

You could lose your money if you put it on the stock market. If you insert it in real estate, you may lose it. If you put money into starting a business, you may lose it.

That is all true.

However, the best ways to supercharge your wealth accumulation are the stock market, real estate, and starting a company. Instead of you need to work hard for your money, they are what let your money begin to work hard for you.

If you play and don't lose, you'll avoid all three of them. You're going to avoid the losses you were afraid of, but sadly, you're going to suffer a worse loss, a loss of opportunity. Safety won't be your reward, but regret.

3) Rich individuals are dedicated to being rich. The poor want to be rich.

They all want to be rich. Few individuals would say that they would rather struggle to get by, given a choice between being poor and being rich.

You need to be committed to it if you want to become rich. Regardless of whether you are ready or not, you must be prepared to take the next step.

You've got to put the work in—the risks you need to take.

Commitment could mean getting up sooner. Instead of catching up on Netflix, it could mean reading a book that will strengthen your mind. Whatever form it takes in your life, tangible signs of your dedication that you can point to should exist. Desire can be all discourse; dedication takes action.

4) Rich individuals think big. The poor think small.

I have a friend who has begun to dabble in the world of online money-making. I speak with him regularly and try to encourage him to keep moving forward. I addressed him recently, and he said that perhaps on the off chance that he stayed with it long enough, he would ultimately have the option to supplant his $35k wage with his online income.

Thirty-five thousand dollars?

He could push the number for him that must have seemed like the highest without me getting on his case for being unrealistic.

What happened was that, for setting the bar so low, I got on his case.

There are several reasons why a big vision is necessary for you. A big vision is more motivating, first of all. You'll invest a ton of energy pondering if it's great on the off chance that you believe you will have to struggle with long periods of working away at your venture to arrive at the purpose of making $35,000/year. On the other hand, if you're shooting for, let's say, ten times that amount, the job you're putting in no longer needs to be justified. The work will pay off in a big way.

Another reason is that it helps you think outside the box by thinking big. Instead of thinking, what should I do to get somebody to buy my $5 ebook? You think, "What would I have to do to get someone to buy an online course for $500?" "(or an online $5,000 course).

Thinking big, finally, stretches you. You are always looking onward and upward rather than becoming complacent.

Right now, are you thinking big or little?

We're coming up with a deadline for a goal I set myself, and I'm going to be a little shorter. I am angry in one sense, but I am super grateful in a deeper sense for setting such a lofty goal. If I didn't set the bar high, I'm way closer to achieving what I want than I would be.

Big dreams. Even if you fall short, you're going to end up way beyond where you would otherwise have been.

5) Rich individuals concentrate on opportunities. Poor individuals concentrate on obstacles.

Have you ever heard someone claim before Uber that they had the idea for Uber? Why did they not do anything about it then? If I had to choose one explanation, this might be it: stuck them in a mentality that recognized barriers, not possibilities.

With Uber, there are plenty of obstacles:

• Why would an unlicensed stranger just trust someone to pick them up? (I even know people who, due to safety concerns, will not use Uber)

• How do you expect the well-established taxi business to compete?

• What about the fact that so many customers are older and are struggling with technology and apps?

Moreover, there are all the challenges inherent in running a company: where will you get funding, what will your business model look like, etc.

If all you can see are obstacles, even if it stares you right in the face, you will never seize on a chance.

Despite their barriers, you need to look for opportunities and have the courage to tackle them.

6) Rich individuals respect other rich and successful people. Poor people resent successful and rich people.

This quote shows one of the rich and poor divisions of the deepest worldview: the mindset of abundance vs. the scarcity mindset.

The mindset of abundance recognizes that you will have to help many other individuals if you want to succeed. As the great Zig Ziglar was known to have said:

"If you just assist others in achieving what they want, you can have everything you want in life."

If you're a self-made millionaire, then it means that many people have taken advantage of your actions, and everybody has won. You consider abundance and achievement like a candle: there's additional for everybody on the off chance that I share some of what I have with you.

If you have a scarcity mindset, on the other hand, you see wealth and success like a pie. There's less left to go around if someone takes a bigger slice than everybody else. If you have a scarcity mindset, then because they were greedy and took too big a slice, you greatly resent people like Oprah, Mark Zuckerberg, and Bill Gates.

If you have a bounty mentality, you respect and try to copy those people. Through their actual work and their charitable donations, you also recognize the value they have brought to the world.

Even as I have begun to develop a mindset of abundance, I can sometimes resent rich people because of envy. I am fighting this by practicing gratitude and reminding myself that comparing where I am on my journey is not fair (plus comparisons are normally bad news anyway unless you compare yourself to your former self).

7) Rich people are associated with successful, positive individuals. Poor people are connected to negative or unsuccessful individuals.

Here's where things are getting real. "Your network is your net worth" has often been saying. It has likewise been seen that "you are normal of the five individuals with whom you invest the most time."

So with whom do you invest your time?

Do they make you better, or do they drag you down?

With their positive vibes, do they invigorate you, or do they suffocate you with their negativity?

The brutal reality is that there is no space for negative vibes if you want to be successful.

That friend who always complains: they either need to stop or find someone else to complain to.

In the world, there's enough negativity. If you need to be successful, you should take a page from the book of the phenomenal business visionary Gary Vaynerchuk: "only positive vibes."

8) Rich individuals are prepared to promote themselves and their worth. Poor individuals think about selling and promotion negatively.

You need to advance yourself and what you have to bring to the table if you need anybody to catch wind of you. It's going to be awkward and awkward, but it's the (only) best way to move forward.

There is nowhere you can escape the need for yourself to be promoted. Regardless of whether you don't attempt to go into business and go up the professional bureaucracy, you'll need to urge yourself to get recruited; you'll need to urge yourself to get an advancement, and so forth.

I'm surely not saying that you ought to be self-important or presumptuous; however, if you have something great to bring to the table, let individuals know about it for the good of their own.

A fear of promotion and selling can do Nothing but hold you back.

9) Rich individuals are larger than their problems. Poor individuals are smaller than their problems.

Have you ever heard someone try to justify why they're not successful when they're not successful? As long as they have an arm, they will have a string of excuses, and all of them will shift the blame to someone or something else. It's the fault of the government. It was the fault of their old boss; The sector is in decline. There is a bad market. Their colleagues are not doing their job etc.

The way they talk about their issues makes you think they're never going to succeed, and their issues are bigger than they are.

Successful individuals understand that their problems are barriers that will have to be tackle for them to continue to succeed. They are bigger in their minds than their problems.

You can choose which of these mindsets you're going to adopt.

10) Excellent receivers are rich people. Poor individuals are poor receivers.
Help you need.

Yes, I believe you have the ability to fulfill your dreams, but you need help. It's keeping you down and should be placed under check if your pride doesn't allow you to find support.

The impact of the strengthening of a relationship is a hidden benefit of receiving. Your perception is probably the opposite of reality if you struggle with receiving: you likely imagine that tolerant something from somebody "places you in their debt," however, it simply makes you nearer to them. If you deny others' help, you pass up a free chance to build a relationship.

I must mention that I do not mean that you should start practicing false humility if you have to keep your pride in check.

Bogus modesty is similarly just about as terrible as pride and squares you from accepting, getting praises and acknowledgment from another huge type of receiving.

You shouldn't hang your head down and mumble about how it wasn't that huge of an arrangement, and you would prefer not to assume an excess of praise when somebody praises you. It isn't humility, and it's posturing. It's worthless to you, and it's offensive to them because you imply that their praise was misdirected somehow.

You should look at the other individual without flinching when you are praised and disclose to them genuinely, "Thank you, I'm respected that you would offer me that praise." It could be harder than the head-down approach, but accepting a compliment requires real humility, and humility is difficult.

11) Based on outcomes, rich people choose to get paid. Based on time, poor individuals choose to get paid.

I say this constantly (pun intended): time is your most valuable asset. You can bring in money while saving time if you invest your time making something that you can sell rather than time. On the off chance that you exchange time for money, you get money and lose time. Based on outcomes, the alternative to being paid for your time is to be paid, which is scary for individuals. That means maybe you'll fail. You may not be able to make the kind of money you need to make (and add insult to injury, which would mean that your job was not good enough, a demoralizing thought). Of course, "it might not work" means "it might work," and if it works, if you stayed stuck trading time for money, the results would be beyond anything you could imagine.

12) Rich individuals think "both." Poor individuals think that "either/or"

It goes back to the mindset of abundance vs. the mindset of scarcity. Do you honestly think both of us can win, or do I have to lose for you to win? Will, we both be able to get what we want, or will it be one or the other? Can we work together to build up each other, or are we destined to fight to tear down each other?

It can apply not only to competition or collaboration areas but also to the way you manage your time and resources.

Should the present or the future be your focus? Both.

Should you concentrate on quantity or quality? Both.

It might appear to be an either/or, and it could be an elusive approach to do both, yet some individuals are doing it.

You may sometimes really have to choose either/or, but it should always be your first thought to ask how you can choose both. I'd add the caveat that does not mean you're never going to have to make a trade-off. You definitely will means that you'll start finding them if you start looking for possibilities for "both."

13) Rich individuals concentrate on their net worth. Poor people concentrate on their income from working.

I want a high income, don't get me wrong, but the problem with focusing only on a high income is that your effort is the only way to make money. You can let your money begin doing some of the work when you take a step back and look at your net worth. To make money, you can use your money. When your expenses are higher, a high income isn't so great. Ideally, you'd live below your means and spend a portion of your income building your net worth, making money using your money.

14) Rich people manage well with their money. Poor individuals are mismanaging their money well.

Consumer debt in the USA is one of the biggest illustrations of this. I remember reading a USA Today article that said that, according to a recent study, as a group, people with the lowest net worth have the highest credit card debt.

When debt is okay, there are times. You should "only borrow to build" is my rule of thumb, meaning you should expect to get a return that outweighs the borrowing cost. Most of the debt on credit is not like this. What happens is that the need to pay is delayed, and you pay a premium for the ability to do so (i.e., interest). It means that you are working to earn money you've already spent when you go to work. That isn't good a job of managing your money as you can do. There are other ways, more subtle, where you can see this dichotomy. I truly believe that rich people are more likely to invest in themselves than poor people are, in order of magnitude. To give them the knowledge and skills required to succeed, they spend money on books and courses. They spend money on starting a company. They invest money into growing their business. Those who truly manage their money well understand that one of the wisest uses of money is to improve yourself.

15) Rich people have to work hard for their money. For their money, poor people work hard.

Rich people put their cash into vehicles that make money: stocks, real estate, a business of their own. More money is earned from their money. Poor people are in debt and have to work longer hours to pay for the money they have already spent.

Much of that is because things that make the most money, in the long run, get little return in the short term.

We all know that you can make a lot of money if you invest early, but when you put away what little you have to spare, you see you hardly earn anything on the stock market. That is because it works that way. In the beginning, you see nearly no results... but then it begins to snowball. It's the same as investing in real estate or starting a company. Lots of unpaid hours and confusion as to whether it's all going to be worth it. Then things will start snowballing. Those who believe in the system will be sufficiently confident to let their money work hard for them. Trust the mechanism.

16) Despite the fear, rich individuals act. The poor let fear stop them.

It is a big one, man, oh man.

Listen, if it were possible to find the things you wanted in life in your comfort zone, you would have already found them.

Things like wealth and achievement require you to take the frightening act of stepping out of your comfort zone and doing the things that will make you succeed. Here I highly recommend that you make your dream greater than your fear. Write down that. Repeat that to yourself again. As often as you can, visualize it. Make it something without which you cannot imagine living. It is painful to face your fear, but if the pain of staying the same becomes greater than the pain of changing, you have an opportunity.

17) Rich people constantly learn and grow. Poor people already think they know.

Each of us has a certain vision of future success that we hope to achieve. The thing here is, the version of you that exists in your vision doesn't just have stuff you want; they know stuff you don't know. If you want things, you first need to look for the knowledge that will get you there.

I still believe that the best way to do this is by reading good books. I heard that Malcolm X was once asked by a reporter what an alma mater was, and he answered "books."

On the StartupCamp podcast, I heard Dale Partridge say that if you're not reading at least six books a year, you're not investing enough in your ongoing education. This year, I'm on pace to read close to 50 books. I believe that 50 in 2022 do not need to be read, but I am sure you will advise him to set himself an aggressive goal.

Finally

When someone usually begins to talk about the importance of mentality, the rejection is "it can't change your mind easily."

The truth is that changing your mind is not easy. Look at the above list; many of the characteristics of "poor" people are beliefs and habits you've never even known about. Many of them are deep insecurities that are difficult to unravel.

Please think of the first item on the list: the rich's belief that they create their lives and the poor's belief that their lives occur. It's easy to believe that you live because it lets you get away from the hook. You don't have to be where you are; your parents, your teachers, bosses, and all the people who did not recruit you for seeing your potential. It is much more painful and difficult to take responsibility for your circumstances than it sounds.

Usually, bad thoughts feel much better in the short term than good ones. So we're defaulting on them.

For some time in a pocket notebook, I've been holding this list of "wealth files," and I often reexamine it. I am progressing to improve my thinking, but a lot of work remains to be done.

For instance, I admire other rich and successful people now and then but from time to time, I find it difficult to get certain people out of jealousy when I get frustrated with my lack of progress. Sometimes I resent those who dared to begin earlier than me. It's so unfair to me, I believe; they're so far past me that I just ought to have started earlier. However, this thinking does no good, and I have to fight to get rid of it.

What areas do you tend to fall in line with "poor" individuals in the above list?

Focus on changing your attitude, and then you can work on changing your actions. From there, the results follow.

Having a healthy mindset is not just critical to wealth accumulation. In virtually every endeavor, it is critical to success.

If the serious pursuit of your dreams does not work, willpower will not work. To keep you coherent over time, you need an unbeatable system. Take sufficient steps forward, and you're going to get where you want to go.

DO I DESERVE THE OPPORTUNITY?

Are you deserving of richness? Good enough for riches, are you?

You know, I believe the answer to these two questions is a resounding **YES!** But, let me ask you this question: do you?

I mean, do you believe that you deserve it?

Even if you're not working hard for this? Even if your family and friends don't have it? Do you need to succeed, even if you are not qualified and have no education (which is what your condition tells you)?

Unless they sweat for it, a lot of people don't believe they deserve wealth. Unless they put 'hard yards' in there, and even then, if everybody else they know and love can't have the same kind of riches, they'll often feel too guilty, even if they feel like they've sweated for it, to let themselves have it.

It is a lot I see.

When I work with customers to help them create more wealth in their lives, one of the biggest blocks I find repeatedly is worth it.

If you suspect that in your life, deep down, you are not entirely deserving of freedom, choice, and abundance... then this may be the very reason why you are struggling financially or are unable to achieve the time you desire for freedom.

Because in shaping your outer experience, your deeply held internal subconscious beliefs about money play a powerful role.

Consider the big picture. We've all have convictions that we came to acknowledge as 'truths' because of our childhood and youth molding. These were normally passed down to us as acquired qualities from our parents, our good examples, and our social and cultural impacts.

Concerning funds, these convictions are regularly communicated in basic truisms, for example, "money doesn't fall from the sky," or "you need to buckle down for your money." Hearing these articulations again and again since early on, we disguise their messages.

These downward beliefs probably became cultural because they protected people against pain, harm, or disappointment in earlier times in history. Times when, for example, there was no middle class, when career paths and life opportunities were very different, and when there were still societal norms that would seem outrageous to us now (slavery, anyone?).

Albeit the world may have proceeded onward from that point forward from multiple points of view. Although we live in a period of extraordinary change (and opportunity!) remotely... a significant number of us keep on hanging on firmly to those equivalent unaltered but then obsolete convictions at an inner mind level.

Often, those beliefs do not serve us anymore. On the contrary, in ways we are not even aware of, they have the effect of holding us back. That's why they're referred to as beliefs that limit.

The path = The Target.

Here's a great question: Why do you need to legitimize any success that may stream into your life by restricting it to the sort that comes from "hard work"?

Why?

If you want freedom, choice, and abundance in your life... does it serve you to believe that struggle, hard work, and sacrifice must be the path to that?

If your assumption about the PATH characteristics is at odds with the DESTINATION characteristics, then the destination will always remain just beyond your reach.

For a minute, ponder that. It is essential. Because here's a little-known truth: there are the same path and destination.

Yep.

And the fastest way to get to a life of freedom, choice, abundance is to believe that NOW, and ALWAYS, those things are available to you... to believe that those things are part of your true path.

Consequently, this will be expressed in your external circumstances NOW and ALWAYS on the off chance that you have a strongly held inclination that you are undeserving of money or if you are not sure that it will come to you effectively. On the other side, if you genuinely accept at a profound, inward level in your deservingness of abundance... at that point, cash has consent to stream into your life effectively NOW and ALWAYS.

In the end, the subconscious mind always prevails. At every stage along the way, it also prevails!

Changing your mindset, changing your reality

How, then, can you shift from a limiting mindset to a solid belief that you deserve financial freedom and can achieve it?

Here's where the real job is. It isn't hard work, and it can be incredibly fast work, but it's vital to work.

Because that's how the path becomes the destination, and your everyday reality becomes abundance: by believing it into being. And the rewards are unbelievable!

Like, how does it sound to you like a life of freedom, choice, and abundance? Hey, want it? Well, you can have it believe me. There's a way to believe this, though, TRULY... which I'm taking you step-by-step through here. If you think you deserve to be rich, even a little bit, take a while to clarify why you should be rich. When asked about this at workshops and conferences by entrepreneurs and professionals, it is clear that a fair number of them believe that they deserve to be wealthy, which is a minimum net worth of $1 million or more, to varying degrees. Dig deeper, four broad justifications exist:

• "I truly, truly wish to be wealthy." Since they intensely desire a wide range doesn't imply they ought to be rich.

• "I'm a good person." They should be rich because of their good deeds and the positive ways they use their wealth.

• "I'm talented and intelligent." They should be rich because of their intellectual prowess or some specialized ability.

• "I know people." They should be wealthy because of their network of relationships.

Whatever bad you want to be rich; no matter what you've done to date and what you plan to do, whether you're brilliant; no matter who you know or who knows you, you NOT deserve to be wealthy, unambiguously, and categorically. But in this regard, you aren't alone. To put it simply, no one deserves wealth. In the question, the keyword is "deserve." Being rich is not a right. It is, at best, a possibility.

Very few individuals are transitioning to wanting to take action when considering the four broad justifications based on empirical research. There are three questions for each justification, which you should probably consider.

"I want to be wealthy."

- How committed to becoming wealthy are you?

- To become rich, what are you willing to sacrifice?

- How does your motivation transform into productive actions?

"I'm a good person."

- How can you translate into personal wealth your values and ideals?

- What are the benefits of getting rich by being "good?"

- What effect does being "good" have on the way you deal with others?

"I'm talented and intelligent."

- How do your skills place you squarely in the money line?

- How likely are you to undertake projects outside of your expertise?

- In other areas, how do you offset your weaknesses?

"I know people."

- How would you say you will use your organization to bring in money?

- How do you make money today from your improved relationships?

- Are the individuals you understand willing to refer you strongly to other individuals you want to meet?

Suppose you have responded positively to each of the questions for a justification that you identify with. In that case, you are moving in the right direction to become a self-made millionaire. It is not always the case, though.

To put it simply, becoming rich is NOT an entitlement. It's neither a privilege nor a right. However, if you are healthy and motivated, the advantage you have is that you are very likely to have the chance to pursue wealth or happiness. It takes advantage of this chance by actively, vigorously, and intelligently pursuing wealth that can potentially become rich.

You're worth it!

THE PRINCIPLES OF GETTING RICH

Hey guys, I've been working with these ideas and tips for over a year. Now I want them to be shared.

So, I'm quite wealthy... More than provided for our needs... And with rich people, I've spent a ton of time. To be rich and build a huge load of abundance, I need to share my principles.

I know now what I was going to ask, is that a RICH GUY? And I would say to that, I'm not a dirty wealthy person, but I am an entrepreneur who is successful and who helps other companies to tax, wealth, and business growth.

My perspective comes from the rich business owners and consultants.

I was lucky that the average person did not have one thing - my first company had a tax and accounting company to grow that helped small enterprises. I have been a strategic tax planner and the company's core developer. I have gone as an owner and handed it over to my business partners after making it an excellent location.

As well as my success and a decent amount of wealth since I am 37 years old, my main advice is that wealthy people guide me, do their tax planning, and am an insider consultant who works for wealthy people.

So I want to speak about the best ways to become legitimately rich, and that's profound, and 11 things shattering the earth came up. :)

I feel that advice on how to get wealthy from the perspective of being an employee is incredibly difficult.

As an employee, you have to be an enterprise owner, ultimately an investor; building high wealth is difficult.

First, learning about wealth quadrants is the key to building wealth.

I've worked with many center American individuals who have acquired between 80 thousand and 250,000 every year - yet I need to discuss what it would take to turn out to be truly rich.

I have worked with truly rich clients, nobody's staff, business owners, and investors.

To become rich, the first thing to do is to;

Learn the quadrant of cash flow

Learn about the cash flow quadrant and move from an employee to an investor and business owner.

Robert Kiyosaki has a publication called the cash flow quadrant - There are four types of earnings - EBSI -

Employee, Self Employed, Business Owner, and Investor.

OPM = "Money for others" or "Time for other people."

4 EBSI Cashflow Quadrants

a: Employee

Staff - means that you have a JOB - there's no leverage here, and you traded hours in the number of dollars out. You have a wage, and you have to put your income into work.

b: Self Employed

Self-worker - no leverage - it is always a time-in, equivalent to money - is essentially a job with more than a worker.

c: Business Owner

Business owners: They use time and money from other people to work and generate income for themselves. You create a system and then organize others to build wealth by using the system. There is a lot of leverage here because you will use other people's time and money to create wealth.

d: Investment person

INVESTOR – again, your wealth does not rely on your own time – so it leverages, but here you are part of the investor class where other systems are purchased to work for you.

LEVERAGE is when time and money from other people start to generate revenue. It's a multiplier by yourself resources of time and money.

Investors and business owners possess the greatest wealth. They not only hold the majority of the world's wealth, but they also enjoy more freedom at lower levels of wealth because the efforts of other people work for you.

Your aim should be to become a business owner and an investor if you want to be rich.

Rich Dad Poor Dad "cash flow quadrant" Robert Kiyosaki

The richest individuals I know are people who have become business owners and investors and use the time, money, and systems of other people to create wealth for themselves. You have reached a point where your system works for you, and you participate because you love or want to add value - not because you have to do all your job yourself.

So that's the first thing - take advantage of your business as a proprietor and ultimately as an investor, but you must climb up the "entrepreneur ladder" to reach it.

2. Climb the Business Owner Ladder

The Entrepreneur Ladder is the business owner/investor quadrant process.

The second thing you need to do to grow rich is to climb the ladder of the entrepreneur.

You will have to climb the entrepreneur's ladder to become a business owner or entrepreneur.

3 Entrepreneurial Stages:

- Technician - Do yourself things

- Manager - Working with your friends

- Employer - Encouraging business management systems and people (think franchise)

You begin self-employed. At that point, you get a few people to work close by you, and you oversee others, which gives influence in your abundance building. Afterward, you'll have to create SYSTEMS and enable PEOPLE around you, so the business tasks occur without you accomplishing the work. The aim is to create a framework that uses the optimal opportunity for others to accomplish the job - which is what the problem is here.

You'll want to come to the point where you are a true businessman but almost always begin as a self-employed technician.

The second part of becoming rich builds on the first part – you'll need to move into the corporate owner and investor quadrants, but to do so, you need to climb the entrepreneur ladder. That means that people or technology building systems and teams can do things.

3. Acquire required self-learning knowledge

Thirdly, the knowledge needed to build a company is to be acquired.

Rich people build businesses and invest, but normally they had to find this knowledge outside the traditional education system.

Learning abroad is where the majority of entrepreneurs know to become wealthy.

What do I mean here? What do I mean here? Most rich people participate in companies that they have not received from a teacher or k-12 education system, usually from employment training and industry skills. Read this article on Job Training versus University training.

Many of the rich people I know built their organization because they got an insider understanding of the market and obsessed about ways to do it better - and afterward ACTUALLY marched out to make those points.

Some Obscure Job Instances

To get rich, become aware, and acquire knowledge in various industries and sectors that offer entrepreneurship, you need to overcome one of the biggest obstacles.

Knowing the various industries and sectors in which people make money does not have to rely on K-12 education or college. Work and startup experiences in these industries are much more helpful, and you need to find mentors to help you become aware of them.

Job Experience & Mentorship are CRITICAL to acquire the required knowledge.

Business is an all-time catch. People make BIZARRE Things for profit. The biggest problem that keeps people poor is that they never know which industries, companies, or activities can profit!

I have intertwined with a few examples of bizarre business.

- Energy brokerage

- Old cheese and milk brokering

- Truck Rebuilds to prevent new Tier diesel criteria

- Bus Services of Hangover

- Recycling of fryer Grease

- Ventilation Restaurant "Hood Cleaners."

- Consultants for Underwriter Labs

- Sales of medical equipment (train doctors how to use cutting edge products)

- Amazing FBA Completion

- Para Planners for Financial Investment Professionals

- Processing of the title

- Tax planning and engineering design for energy efficiency

- Sales and consultancy home remodeling

I know very dumb folks get rich because they have found a niche or become conscious of a sector where high profits are possible.

In every service, people make money, brokerage, niche industries, etc.

The wealth is in the niches, and your system of k-12 education is **INCAPABLE** to help you identify important things. They are professors who have gone down the predictable, noble, and yet burgeoning career path. They teach good qualifications, go to college, get licenses for teachers, and work in that self-perpetuating system. Once again, you can't rely on teachers or training – you need to have the first-hand experience in any industry you are curious about, and you need to have a perspective through books and mentors. It would help if you learned about business opportunities... but not to help you build a rich wealth or help you become aware of the possibilities of business...

The educators are good people, but they are FAR in America if they use their summers and time to manage a business or manage their investments. They are great people.

Our education system is designed to equip you with the foundations, but the best learning can do outside the school if you are willing.

Many of my successful business owners were media students, but they wanted to work with their hands and the hustle and bustle. They took jobs in industries that gave them the experience and the prospect of eventually running their store rather than going to college. They now have a fleet of tractors building homes, huge insurance brokerages, or a property rental company.

MY FACTOR IS THAT YOU WILL CERTAINLY CONTINUE TO BE OBLIVIOUS Of what it requires rich as long as you depend on k-12 and even k-16 education.

So rich people build companies, climb the ladder of the entrepreneur and acquire the knowledge they need

4. Mentoring and Masters intentional perspective

The following thing that rich individuals do - or have done - is that they get intentional about mentorship and seeking after authority in their specialties.

Almost ALWAYS, rich business owners pursue mastery.

They try to learn all that is to be learned in their field.

Whether informal or formal, a good mentor can help you find the perspective needed to master and learn from some secret niches and even industry secrets. One of the key factors is to find a mentor who can help you...

Make it your goal to find people who can be a formal mentor or even as a friend you regularly take to learn about coffee.

Coffee appointments can provide opportunities for mentoring.

Coffee appointments provide me with every valuable perspective; every time - I never told them what I did - I've been able to take their advice and perspectives into my mind. And become better by having coffee with hundreds of successful entrepreneurs throughout the time...

Locate an entrepreneur - or a pioneer at an organization in the kind of business you'd prefer to become, and simply pose them great questions.

Ask them about a 1-hour espresso arrangement and tell them that you're impressed with what they're doing, and you'd love to hear the story and find out more... Come arranged with questions, a notepad, and listen eagerly.

Remember - this is **NOT ABOUT YOU** - this is about them. Don't be a tool to make them look yours... you want to find their secrets!

THE TRICK HERE - do not chat much - ask questions - take **FANTASTIC NOTES** - and attempt to understand the basics and the nuances of their procedures and market.

IF YOU DO THAT WITH 2-10 individuals this year - you'll be light years over where you are today.

There is a big difference between owners of companies who work hard to gain insights from peers and industry experts and people who think they know it all.

GET PERSPECTIVE, GET A MENTOR, and are obsessed by learning all the wise people who are already down the company owner's path.

Okay, so much for **SUMMARY:**

ALRIGHT – let's just shift some gears.

5. Don't spend time on wasteful gambling

The wealthy people I've met don't spend their time on wasteful recreation.

Sure they refuel and re-energize; however, they invest their energy carefully because they comprehend that time is the lone really limited asset we have.

Want to be wealthy? Don't SPEND your precious nonsense time! Typically, rich people don't waste their valuable time on leisure, or if they do, it's AFTER they've accomplished everything they need to do, or it's once they've sacrificed to get their business where it needs to be.

Spend your time wisely and by dreaming and planning, put it to work! Rich people are constantly scheming, planning, and curious about their activities!

Make your new video game planning strategic and tactical.

I know that wealthy people and business owners entertain themselves by working on issues, thinking through plans, and then working on them.

If other people are vegetables in front of a T.V., productive books, listening to a speaker or an audiobook, problem-solving, side hustling, training, planning, or writing are read by rich and successful entrepreneurs.

Think about a video game - for the most part, you are solving problems and puzzles.

Make it a game of wrapping your mind around issues and mapping strategic plans...

DON'T WASTE TIME on wasteful leisure and MENTAL ENERGY.

You need leisure, of course, to relax and get some marginal time.

But to become rich, you should write down your business plans and make them permanent, and then constantly tinker with them to make them better.

You have to forfeit on the off chance that you have a family, and you're an entrepreneur seeking to grow and become a true business visionary. Put your family over the business, yet understand that you need to use however much of your time and thinking as could reasonably be expected to be profitable if you need to be rich.

You know, I place enormous value on execution, in other words, JUST GETTING THINGS DONE, but it's extremely important to plan strategically and tactically.

Time is the lone asset that is FINITE - and if you need to be rich, figure out how to reclaim TONS of your recreation time from thoughtless amusement to critical thinking and business arranging - OR, in any event, acquiring new skills...

It would help if you had time to spare, but too many poor people are dumping their lives into wasteful recreation.

If you need to be rich - don't invest your valuable energy on inefficient recreation - you need to put your brain towards "upward and forward" things like critical thinking or arranging.

Next, well, here's the sixth thing you've got to do to be rich...

6. Develop as a manager and leader

You'll need to develop your leadership & management skills to be wealthy and a great business owner.

Your ability to create a company depends on your ability to be a great manager and a great leader and to develop this leverage that we keep mentioning.

Recollect that E-Myth ladder? You will attempt to amass a group, and a system, to achieve work and build abundance for you, which implies you'll require the abilities to achieve that and become the kind of individual that others need to follow.

Wealthy people are entrepreneurs - normally, they are not self-employed. The difference is that, with resources, they organize other individuals to achieve work.

Unless you have developed the management and leadership skills to move a team along with you, you can **NOT LEVERAGE** up the entrepreneur ladder.

Management is to achieve things through other individuals and resources.

Leadership - a compelling vision, moving forward - influence people towards a preferential future

Leadership is influence, and great leaders move individuals towards a compelling vision.

You need a compelling vision to be a great leader, and you need integrity, love, and John Maxwell-type skills to unleash people and make them want to be next to you on the team...

A great leader creates a vision and manages it properly so that everyone in the team works to pursue that vision...

Suppose you need to be rich by using others' time and money to benefit your organization. In that case, you need to put resources into your leadership and management - so tune in to book recordings by the greats like John Maxwell, Henry Cloud, Jim Collins, Ken Blanchard - and a host of others...

You want to be rich - if you're a great leader, you'll get there faster.

If you need to be an extraordinary pioneer, you need to tune in to books, get the point of view, and get mentors.

The seventh thing to do to be wealthy:

7. Perform, persist, and pursue constant improvement

Rich people understand that success comes from Execution x Persistence x Continuous Improvement

It's tied in with GETTING IT DONE, doing that determinedly, and afterward like turning into an astounding b-ball player - you need instructing, feedback, reviewed input, penetrating, investigation, and scrutinizing. You need to seek after constant improvement taking all things together parts of your life and business.

You will act like the rich if you work on these three things - execution, persistence, and continuous improvement.

Ray Crock - the person who took the Mcdonald's siblings from a top-notch burger joint to the biggest eatery establishment in the universe, put a specific incentive on perseverance.... Here's one of his statements: He said:

"Nothing on the planet can happen of perseverance. Talent won't; Nothing is more normal than ineffective men with Talent. Virtuoso won't; unrewarded virtuoso is very nearly a saying. Education won't; the world is brimming with taught vagabonds. Industriousness and assurance alone are transcendent. "

On the off chance that you need to be rich - that implies you need **GRIT**, you need steadiness, you need to push through failure, dismissal, and discouragement and weariness.

But do you notice that I'm saying three things? I think persistence is not sufficient - if you want to become rich, you also need high execution, persistence, and continuous improvement.

Toyota is famously embracing what is known as Kaizen, the continuous improvement method. Toyota and the six lean sigma movements are meant to teach us - we must always strive to make our companies better.

You must embrace the continuous improvement, or kaizen approach, which every year is obsessed with improvement if you want to be rich and build a business.

So that was number 7... you need to **EXECUTE**, be persistent, and pursue continuous improvement if you want to be rich.

8. By leaving a good "wake," get along with people

You need to coexist with individuals when conducting; on the off chance, you need to be wealthy.

It is possible to boil life down to two key things; how you relate to individuals and how you do things.

As we go through life, we all leave a wake, just as a hot wake leaves a wake as it moves across the water.

Henry Cloud is an author and a psychologist, and he suggests that we're leaving a wake behind us as we go through life... on the one hand, it's how we leave people feeling, and on the other, our ability to perform tasks.

It is about becoming a terrific individual. When we can leave those around us feeling uplifted, good, and valued, richness is sustained and often created faster.

Try to leave a great wake as you relate to individuals and get things done if you want to be truly rich.

9. Reality & Awareness Seek (E.Q.)

SEEK REALITY - combat your need for confidence and search for the reality of how things are.

Rich people are pushing the bull-crap past.

What is that bull-crap I'm talking about?

EQ360 is the best awareness exercise I've ever seen.

My wife and I went out the other day to eat, and there was no good food or services. After the owner came up and said, "how was everything," we said "fine" nicely, and we went on our way.

We're not going back - and the owner thought things were all right. But they completely missed the mark in reality.

It's fine to have that happen to you if you're the server; however, if that eatery proprietor needs to be rich, he needs to battle through and find the REALITY of what's happening.

That's my final piece of non-money advice on how to get rich.

There's no need for affirmation for successful people, and they don't have thin skin. They constantly pursue the truth about things and recognize all warts in life and business that need fixing.

It means that a great business owner finds creative ways to get genuine feedback from customers or surveys individuals to get honest feedback.

If there is one thing that rich people know, it's not helpful or profitable to live in bull-crap land, so they're ruthless in their pursuit of the truth, and they take full ownership of it all — and try to improve it. It is part of the continual improvement side of things.

You should not indulge yourself; you should not encourage yourself to remain ignorant of how you leave people feeling and how you accomplish things. Take a mindfulness workout, get a few books about enthusiastic knowledge, and assist yourself with working with yourself AND your business.

10. Avoid debt & only use it to generate revenue

Avoid debt at all costs and use it to generate income only for calculated leverage.

Rich people use debt ONLY to appreciate assets or assets that produce income. DUMB IS DEBT

Rich people know that there are two kinds of individuals in this world, those who pay interest and those who earn interest.

Rich people don't stupidly use debt; they leverage themselves when they use it to generate more revenue.

Poor people go into debt because of new furniture, a house too big, or vehicles they don't need.

Loaning $10,000 for a boat...Vs... Loaning $10,000 for an excavator to turn your lawn service business into a landscaping company... is what I'm talking about.

Borrowing $10,000 vs. toys and home remodel for an eCommerce website & inventory.

Get out of debt if you want to be rich, and stay there.

And here's the last thing wealthy people are doing...

11. Give, Spend, Save and Save

Give, save expenditure, and accept compounding interest.

Rich people aren't spending all they have. They save a percentage, they give a percentage, and the rest of them live on.

They regulate their spending, give generously to those in need and causes greater than themselves, and recognize the power of interest compounding.

Each rich individual I know has speculation accounts that will exploit accumulating revenue, loaded up with ventures. Open a Vanguard account and start buying s&p 500 or mutual funds based on dividends and get the mathematics of compounding interest working in your favor!

That's what I learned about getting rich, and I'm hoping it will help you out!

HOW TO HAVE THE THOUGHT PROCESS OF BECOMING RICH

It may not be known to you, but your thoughts can influence your life. Thoughts are objects. Scientists have measured the vibrations of people's thoughts and emotions, and they have found that positive, happy thoughts vibrate very quickly, such as love and appreciation. Thoughts such as fear, frustration, and envy vibrate very slowly, however. The Law of Attraction phenomenon explains the connection, even your financial situation, between your thoughts and life. You must first know the ideas you have about money to be rich. If you find that you have any negative thoughts, you need to change them ASAP if you want to become rich. Here are eight ways that you can do this.

1. Trust that you're worthy.

Many individuals have low self-esteem in our culture. We are constantly pestered with "not good enough" messages. Whether you contrast your charm to supermodels or your checking account to Oprah's, you require to think that you truly have something to offer the world. You've got a special gift and talent to help you get rich. It's not a problem for rich people to promote themselves, their services, or their business. That's because they think that they're worthy. You've got to think so, too.

2. Believe that you can.

How often did you hear your parents make statements like, "Money doesn't grow on trees." Or, "Do you believe I'm super-rich?" Many of us have been contrarily modified to feel that money is scant. It isn't. There is a lot of money out available for whoever gets there first. You simply need to accept that merit your "slice of the pie." Anything is conceivable. However, you need to accept that before it occurs.

3. Appreciate what you have already.

If you sit down thinking, "I do not like my house, I wish I have one larger," you send down negative vibration with your thoughts, "I can't wait to get a new car because I'm embarrassed to drive that one." The Law of Attraction states that negative, moveable thoughts do not create a positive thing. You have to love your house or car instead. Or just thanks for having a roof on your head, a bed in, or food on your table. The more appreciation you give to what you have, the higher the chance you will get more.

4. For rich people, be happy.

People hear negative statements about rich people sometimes. If you heard this growing up a lot, your subconscious mind is programmed with negative thinking about rich people. Make any of these sounds familiar: "Rich people are snobs" or "Rich people are not honest," or "Rich people are selfish." And because you certainly don't want to be a "snob," "dishonest," or "selfish," your subconscious probably won't let you become rich. Instead, you realize that many rich people are very good human beings. Believe that what they have deserves it. Bless them, and say in advance, 'thank you,' for getting yourself rich.

5. Use boards of affirmations or vision.

Writing out positive statements (affirmations) and repeating them in your mind over and over again helps your brain to reprogram. "If you discovered in #4 that you think rich people are snobs, then repeat a statement like, "Rich people are kind, kind, and loving people. "I am grateful that someday I will be one of them." Vision boards are also helpful. Get a poster board and cut out what you want from words and pictures. It might be a new car, a big house, a private jet, or a yacht of your own. It is appropriate to place anything that feels good and gets you excited on the board. For maximum results, use your affirmations and your vision board together.

6. Love money.

I heard people say, 'I hate money! I hate money! And it always drops my jaw to the floor. How can money hate you? Well, the reason they hate money is that they have none at all. That doesn't mean that they HATE money. All the hate is the LACK of money. So when you keep saying negative things about money, you need to catch yourself. Turn them around and say to them, "I love money!" My friend is money! It brings me great happiness! The more you place the positive vibrations of love on the subject of money, the more it will be acquired.

7. Be happy to have your bills paid.

I'm sure you had a stomach pit before when you were paying the bills. Most people do. That is because their concentration is on the negative. Everything they're thinking about is how much money is going out, not coming in. But that you need to reframe. When you pay your bills, be happy. Because what, guess? That means you've got the money to pay them! If you didn't pay them, that would mean you had no money at all. So be thankful that you have the cash to payout. It provides you with, after all, a place to live, a car to drive, and food on your table. It's a nice thing!

8. Commit to being rich.

Finally, you need to decide to be wealthy! Do not take no for a reply! Hey, don't give up! To achieve something in life, you must commit yourself to do anything in life. You can't just treat "getting rich" as a hobby or something you're just going to try out and see what happens. That way, it doesn't work. Rich individuals are dedicated to doing whatever it takes to make and keep the money! You've got to do the same. Commit yourself to your objective of being rich, and it will be yours.

WILLPOWER AS A STRENGTH

Nothing can replace perseverance on the earth. Skill will not: Nothing with ability is more natural than fruitless men. Genius won't: a genius unrewarded is just a saying. Education won't: with trained cast-offs, the future is filled. All-powerful is tirelessness and assurance alone. Coolidge, Calvin.

Willpower

You will need self-discipline on the off chance that you will be successful in every area. You should detach yourself from where you are, beat latency and get away from pace!

Originally, the term escape velocity was coined concerning rockets blasting into orbit. They needed sufficient power to escape the gravitational pull of the earth. Similarly, getting a new company off the ground, setting up automated profit-generating systems, or getting ahead requires strong focus and dedication to get the company airborne, a very strong push.

From where does willpower come?

What makes you motivated? It's very hard to make yourself do it if something doesn't inspire you. Every step becomes heavier, more effort is required for everything. Yet if you know you have to do something to get things you want badly, you're going to find the willpower to do what's needed.

As the saying goes: "No lazy people, there are only people who are not sufficiently motivated by the goals they set themselves."

And where do the objectives come from? Uh, dreams! Willpower, ultimately, comes from dreams. At the end of the tunnel, they are the "light," the thing that keeps you going.

Therefore, amazingly, the first step in gaining willpower is to dream of a great dream that inspires and motivates you. The desire to achieve, and the energy to overcome obstacles, will come from this place.

Dreams

On the off chance that you can fantasize- - and not make dreams your master—Rudyard Kipling

Due to society's conditions, trying to dictate our desires makes it often hard to dream clearly.

We are supposed to want this, or that... and often we have to seem to have the right set of desires and be made of the right stuff to be socially accepted.

In many cases, people's real dreams are pushed out of them one way or another by society.

What other people want, you don't have to want. Be free to dream a dream of your own and to imagine the future you want, personally.

Also, desire is often created in us by businesses trying to convince us to buy things. We are presented with powerfully seductive imagery that works on our emotions, constantly telling us that to be happy, appreciated, loved, we want or need certain things.

In these words, it is important for one or the other to stay in touch or to get back in touch with our real dreams along these lines. Ask yourself this: What might you do on the off chance that you realized you were unable to fizzle? Make a rundown. Pull out all the stops. These are your "genuine dreams." Concluding that you will go for your genuine dreams and zeroing in on them will give us the internal strength we need to get them going. The drive. While on the off chance that you are not satisfied with the thing you are doing and why you won't bring the stores to push with all your will.

Dreams should be "unlimited": one of the things many people experience is that their dreams are limited. I'll never accomplish that," they say, and then fall into apathy or a sort of subtle despondency that is carried around as heaviness and lack of excitement." Yet what would you do if you understood you could not fail?

Importance of goal setting

Set a clearly defined aim for yourself. If there was no defined goal, the commitment you have made will force you to be creative, to work harder, and to be more economical than you would have done.

The concept here is that you will come up with it if you have to come up with a certain amount of money each month. If you have to finish a certain project by a certain date, you will do it, whereas the work will "expand to fill the available time" if there is no deadline.

"Pay yourself first" is a very simple way to do this, allocating a certain amount of money to asset investment every month. Through standing order, you can do this so that the money is debited automatically (i.e., to your savings account), and so the money needs to be made! It is your dedication and your aim. It should be enough, but not so much that you hurt yourself, to push you and make you sweat just a bit.

A commitment to finishing a certain project and not letting up until you have done so could be another form of commitment.

A clearly defined objective is a tremendously valuable instrument for making something happen and achieving results. Instead of just telling yourself that you're going to do something, putting yourself in a position where you have to do it achieves much better results.

Temptation Resist

Resisting temptation is another thing you will need to learn. The mind is a trickster, and if possible, always loves to take the easy option. By creating an excuse not to get down to your job and the stuff you really should be doing, it will tempt you... Unless you are hyper-vigilant, you will find yourself drifting into easier, less demanding tasks or even taking the day off!

The best way to resist temptation is to be very goal-oriented and work at any time on the most important task you should do.

Other authors on this subject have mentioned using a "success six" technique, where you write the six most important things to do on a piece of paper... but I'm not necessarily in favor of that. It does get some results, but you may or may not have six tasks that need to be done of primary importance!!

I just rundown all the significant undertakings required to be performed and focus on doing the main errand out of nowhere.

Naturally, tasks organize themselves and press for your attention. Zeroing in on the undertakings that will get results and focusing on them is vital.

As to which tasks are the most important, this can be a challenge to figure out sometimes. The main point here is that certain actions lead to real outcomes and that other actions do not have much significance. Resist the desire to work on whatever seems simple or pleasant, and work on the things that will bring the greatest advantage. Such work will not necessarily be nice or comforting, but the work results will be the job.

Discomfort Management

Willpower training requires an understanding of what I call "managing your level of discomfort." If you are learning a new ability of any kind, you are faced with the task of doing something difficult in some way, and therefore uncomfortable. Your mind will "react" to this discomfort and try to find ways of doing the job. To persist, you have to be determined and have willpower. Yet you also need to "balance" the discomfort; you don't want to be so frantic with willpower that you hurt yourself. Or get sick by pushing too hard or "over-training,"- so it's important to manage the level of discomfort and push yourself to achieve success consistently and sufficiently, but not so hard to cause yourself harm.

Just how much discomfort is "the correct quantity" is something that does not seem to be commonly taught, but it can safely say that most do not push themselves hard enough. Peak performance is not a line that goes up into infinity in any field; it is a curve.

Laziness, poor focus, inattentiveness, and lack of determination are on one side of this curve. Despair, over-training, grasping for success, and calamity are on the other side. It will be one of the trainer's tasks if you have specialist sports training to maximize performance while preventing injury.

DRIVING YOURSELF TO ACT CORRECTLY

They say, "Fake it until you do it." "Dress for the job you're looking for."

A few Americans acknowledge it, purchasing architect logo packs and shoes that they can not bear or dishing out for an extravagance vehicle when they need to attempt to make payments as a Uber driver. (Apparently, this is one thing in L.A. My Uber Mercedes driver told me so)

Well, they've got everything wrong. If you want to be and think of yourself as a wealthy person, surveys show how much you have in your bank account - not your belongings. Here are the things that wealthy Americans think and do that you can copy to enhance your economic position:

They don't splurge.

The rich and famous lifestyles, or the younger sibling, Cribs, would lead us to believe the wealthy like everything they touch to look like an accessory to the Louis XIV palace. But, in reality, with their luxury purchases, the wealthy can be quite conservative. Yes, some people like their Mercedes, Lexus, and BMW, earning more than $250,000. However, a full 61% opt for basic models like Honda, Acura, Volkswagen, and Toyota. Ferrari did not make the top 10. It is upheld by research showing that individuals of high status don't want to spend a lot of money on extravagance items.

"It's cooler among the privileged to buy fewer classic, high-quality products that whisper their origin, rather than many trendy items that shout, "I paid so much for this!"

They value schooling.

You might look at Zuckerberg and wonder if there is even a need for a college degree. But this exception shows the rule: education is essential. In a 2014 Spectrum survey of investors with a net worth of $25 million or more, 82 percent cited education, the second most important factor after hard work, as a factor in building their wealth. And anyway, before he dropped out, academic achievement is what got Zuckerberg to Harvard. Within the U.S. Trust survey, respondents said the most important value emphasized by their family growing up was an academic accomplishment. Studies underline this, with the significance of a graduate and undergraduate degree becoming increasingly important for wealth accumulation. In 2013, one in 110 families with no high school diploma is at least 1 million dollars in wealth, compared to 1 in 2.6 for professional/graduate students in the case of families with no high school degree.

They earn their money rather than inherit it.

In contrast to popular opinion, the wealthy were not necessarily born that way. Only 10 percent of their wealth was inherited in a 2016 U.S. Trust survey for 684 citizens with investable assets over $3 million (that is, not cars or homes, for instance). They earned about half of their money, and 32 percent came from investments.

They believe in hard work.

In a 2014 survey of investors with $25 million or more in net worth by Spectrum, respondents overwhelmingly attribute their achievement to hard work (87 percent), while only 66 percent of respondents cited luck. Experts who have studied the impact of luck on wealth posit that hard work is essential to success; although luck can have a real impact on your earnings for life, perhaps more than most successful individuals would like to admit.

However, other studies show that today's wealthy people work longer hours than low-income Americans (rather than, harking back to the eighteenth century when the gentry lived off crafted by serfs) and spend less time engaging in leisure activities such as watching T.V. To sum up the research: you can work hard and not get rich (see: social workers, teachers), but without working hard, it's much harder to become wealthy.

Never do they feel like they "made it."

Maybe because they feel so far from the finish line, which always seems to be on the distant horizon, is why the wealthy work hard. In a 2013 survey, four out of every ten Americans with an investment of $5 million or more call themselves wealthy. As this enlightening article on the super-rich shows' anxiousness shows, there will always be someone who has a yacht bigger than you.

They're conservatively investing.

Please don't try copying the strategy of the Wolf of Wall Street. Instead of playing the market, wealthy investors with at least $3 million in investable assets tend to favor a relaxed investment approach: high net assets financial investors made their greatest speculation gains through long haul purchase and-hold procedures (86%), conventional stocks, and securities (89%), and a progression of little successes

(83%), as opposed to tossing their assets into huge venture risk methodologies (86%).

Two-thirds of investors with investable assets in the range of $500,000 to $1 million are investing in exchange-traded funds (ETFs) that are merely trying to track the market or a particular market sector. (You see investments in hedge funds and startups as you get into the ultra-wealthy, but that's not available to the average investor.) And approximately half of the rich investors invest in real estate, agricultural land, and woodland assets, which generate consistent, long-term revenues.

They also invest in long-term relationships.

Eighty-six percent were in a drawn-out relationship in the U.S. Trust study, contrasted with not exactly 50% of grown-ups in the U.S. Of those in the overview, 75 percent had their first life partner wedded. That means 65% were married, never divorced, in the survey as a whole. It's no wonder divorces are costly affairs.

HOW TO ACT IN THE MOST EFFICIENT MANNERS

Manners Matter.

When you're around people, you have to know how to act and do certain things. Thomas Corley writes.

"Independent tycoons have dominated certain standards of manners that help them in social settings."

Will dominating these manners propensities ensure a fortune? Not. Yet, it unquestionably will not do any harm.

They send thank you cards.

"Saying thank you is an impression of your character," Corley composes. "Don't Facebook them, Tweet them, Instagram them. Send a note to say thanks."

When do the rich compose cards to say thanks, and when would it be advisable for you too? At the point when somebody recalls your birthday, it alludes a customer to you, acquaints you with an important contact, or helps you or a relative out.

They remember the little details.

Rich individuals recall others' birthday events, leisure activities, interests, schools joined in, main youth residences, and names of their life partners and children.

The little details matter, Corley stresses. They permit you to build friendships with other achievement disapproval of individuals, a foundation for rich individuals. "Assemble as much information about your connections as possible," he composes. "The more you think about individuals you draw in with, the more ammo you'll have in your arsenal to assist you in adequately speaking with them."

They have good table manners.

"In all honesty, the vast majority don't have the foggiest idea how to eat," Corley composes. Be that as it may, "In the grown-up universe of the successful people, you need to realize how to eat at social settings."

It implies putting your napkin on your lap when you plunk down, holding off on beginning until everybody has their food, eating at a similar speed as the rest of the table, sitting straight up, and pardoning yourself when you're done.

They know how to dress.

"Dress for progress" is more than an infectious saying. Corley says there's a foolproof method to dress for work, prospective employee meetings, weddings, and formal or casual meals - and rich individuals have dominated it.

Truth be told, as Business Insider's Dennis Green writes, "Studies have shown that wearing decent garments in the workplace can influence how individuals see you, how sure you're feeling, and even how you're ready to think conceptually."

In one examination, "Those dressed inadequately (in warm-up pants and plastic shoes) arrived at the midpoint of a hypothetical benefit of $680,000, while the gathering dressed in suits amassed a normal benefit of $2.1 million," Green reports. "The gathering dressed impartially found the middle value of a $1.58 million benefit."

They introduce themselves properly.

The greater part of us doesn't feel certain about our capacity to give a legitimate handshake. Well-off individuals are not just skilled to execute a successful handshake. They have mastered different guidelines regarding making presentations - they smile, visually connect, and pose a lot of questions about the other individual, Corley explains.

"In life, you will be constrained into circumstances where you will meet new individuals," he writes. "This is a chance to create important connections. Some might be your next boss, future mate, next closest companion, future associate, financial backer, or future colleague."

Furthermore, initial introductions matter more than you may assume.

GETTING INTO THE RIGHT INDUSTRY

I've never met any individual who would not like to bring in more money; in any event, when they imagine about it, their activity regularly parts with them. You needed advanced education to have the option to bring in more money from your work. To get a quality education with someone else paying the money, you look for scholarships. Your parent needed you to go to school, get passing marks and find a decent work line, with the goal that you can take in substantial income and live a superior life. The world framework has been worked around money. Furthermore, the individuals who attempt to deny this frequently fall casualty of this framework.

So what are the absolute most ideal approaches to situate yourself to draw in more money? You can either choose to pursue a career in archaeology blindly or look for more opportunities to create wealth. What's more, on most occasions, the ideal approach to distinguish openings is to follow the money. You pose the inquiry which businesses have created the most riches. Which ventures are the quickest developing? Addressing questions like these can guide you in the correct spots toward build up your fundamental advantages and energy. Let's check out the industries that have developed one of the most tycoons today.

Financial Services

The financial service industry has made the most number of moguls since current occasions, as indicated by the Wealth Report. A great deal of money is made occupied with money. Individuals and organizations gifted in sending and developing money are behind the best endeavors on the planet today.

Consider the big picture, all the money individuals make on the planet is overseen by a financial institution; it very well may be a commercial bank, investment bank, a Hedge Fund, Insurance, or an abundance portfolio. Also, when individuals execute their money, it's as a rule through some financial institution. The establishment of the whole world's economy is based on the money industry. The majority of the monetary emergency in history frequently started from the money industry, like the 2008 Global Financial Crisis. In like manner, the vast majority of the world's monetary successes are connected to the money industry.

No big surprise, many fintech startups are jumping up today like FlutterWave, Mpesa, Bamboo, CowryWise, and numerous others. Money innovation startups draw in Africa's most investment financing than in some other classification. The money industry holds immense freedom to make riches. Also, it utilizes a large number of individuals across the mainlands.

Technology

Technology comes close to financial services for making the highest number of tycoons. Indeed, the two enterprises are the impetus to the next. The marriage between the financial service area and technology has made huge abundance like nothing considered before it. Furthermore, the two enterprises are the driving force of different ventures today.

Technology, specifically, has played out well in possession of the younger age. I can't envision what the degree of joblessness would have been in a universe of more than 7 billion individuals without technology. Furthermore, on the off chance that you consider the incubate financial climate in this piece of the world, it would have been a calamity without the chances technology has accommodated the younger age. Indeed, no other industry makes abundance as quick as the technology industry. Take, for example, Zoom—established zoom in 2011. After nine years, it is worth more than the main seven carriers in the United States joined and has made the organizer a tycoon. A portion of these carriers has been around for more than 50 years. Take a gander at the highest esteemed organizations on the planet today. Six out of the main 10 are technology organizations.

The fascinating thing about the technology industry is that it cuts across each industry. The agric area needs technology just as the money, media, wellbeing, and retail industry. It additionally has space for innovative, specialized deals and backing faculty. There is a spot for everybody in the technology space.

Real Estate and Construction

Real estate is the most seasoned wellspring of abundance all through the ages. The sanctuary is a need of life, regardless of whether for private or commercial purposes. It makes real estate one of the most seasoned and most comprehensive ventures for making riches. By comprehensive, I imply that it is available to however many individuals will be a piece.

Most affluent individuals either got well off from real estate or developed their abundance from real estate. The real estate industry has a broad worth chain from property obtaining to development, support, the board, proficient services, advanced security, and other related exercises. On the off chance that you are hoping to develop your abundance, you can't turn out badly with real estate.

Food and Beverages

The world has more than 7 billion mouths to take care of. By 2030, we'll have an extra 1 billion. Furthermore, by 2050, we'll be taking a gander at around 9.7 billion mouths to take care of day by day. We are not yet creating sufficient food to take care of everybody on the planet enough. As more individuals are pulled out of poverty, we'll have more individuals requesting quality food and refreshments to burn-through. It doesn't take basic intuition to see the potential in the food and drink industry. I've by and by put resources into an agribusiness for more than three years now and can say that this industry holds gigantic freedoms.

Notwithstanding whatever is going on the planet: pandemic, wellbeing or financial emergency, environmental change, or catastrophic events, there is one unassailable reality about people. We should eat and drink. To build your career around the food and beverage industry, you won't be wrong.

Health

Regardless of where you reside, we would all be able to concur on a certain something; health is riches. This COVID-19 worldwide pandemic has drawn this fact out into the open more than everything else lately. On the off chance that the health industry is undermined, all the other things come disintegrating down. The worldwide Pharmaceutical industry is valued at over a trillion dollars. However, that is only a piece of the health area. The drawback is that the health area is more directed than most different areas for valid justifications. Regardless, the health area offers gigantic freedoms to make huge riches.

Media and Entertainment Industry

Avengers: End game netted more than $2.79 billion from dramatic income alone. Yet, you don't need to be just about as large as Marvel studios to profit from this industry. The tools and media outlet's greatest fascination is about the most minimal section boundary than some other computerized media technology industry. It doesn't depend on academic qualifications, either. Indeed, even the most exceedingly terrible understudy in school can become showbiz royalty in this area. Yet, I'll need to concede that these can be drawbacks because the low section boundary implies greater rivalry and more trouble to stick out.

Regardless, in the media and entertainment industry, there is a lot of money to be made. Individuals will consistently need to be engaged or become more acquainted with what's going on external to their current circumstances. Movies, music, computer games, TV, and the advances that empower them are treasure troves if you can be adequately inventive to stick out.

Renewable Energy

I utilize an inverter system at home and the workplace. However, just around one of every 15 or 20 people I meet utilizes renewable energy. Numerous people trust it's costly. They may not realize that it is less expensive than running and keeping a generator over the long haul. If I somehow happened to begin another business today, I will think about solar and inverter deals and establishment; and spotlight my marketing on educating people on the distinction in incentive between utilizing a generator and an inverter. There is a huge market for renewable energy sources, particularly in non-industrial nations where the public force supply is untrustworthy.

This post isn't to urge you to seek after a career or business basically because you trust it will get you the most cash-flow. Discover the harmony between productivity and interest. Don't simply pick a field given energy or money. It's more brilliant to consider commercial incentives just as what intrigues you.

CAUTIONS

"Order the individuals who are rich in this current age not to be haughty, nor to trust in questionable riches however in the living God, who gives us richly everything to appreciate."

What rings a bell when you consider rich individuals? A finely dressed man? A colossal, luxurious house? The huge staff of workers? Vehicles? Adornments? This picture might be the explanation that Bible alerts to the rich so regularly go unnoticed. The Christian in 21st century America is surprisingly well off. Regardless of whether we have, however, a little by American principles, we have undeniably more than most in our reality and would put individuals of Bible occasions to disgrace. So it is to individuals like us that God cautions: "Order the individuals who are rich in this current age not to be haughty, nor to trust in questionable riches however in the living God." Allow us to consider this notice one given to rich individuals like us.

Paul is educating Timothy of what he should show different individuals from the congregation, and he advises him to order the "rich in this current age not to be haughty." "Haughty" here is likewise interpreted as "honorable" and "conceited"; God is cautioning us first against the common inclination to get cocky. The verifiable duplicity of abundance is that the individuals who have it are preferable individuals over the most certainly not. It isn't new. At the point when Jesus cautioned that "it is simpler for a camel to experience the aperture of a needle than for a rich man to enter the realm of God," the witnesses were surprised, pondering who could be saved. James cautioned of Christians treating rich individuals better than poor, giving them consideration and honor. Perhaps most important is the story of Jesus about the rich man and Lazarus as it shows a homeless person as the legend while torturing the rich man! The scriptural perspective on riches is that they are, best-case scenario, a snag to defeat as we continued looking for paradise positively, not something to be arrogant about! God gives us all that we have, so we should see our abundance given to us as stewardship, to be used in the best way before returning to the expert. The caution isn't to be haughty-not to think we have procured what we have, that we are superior to others since we have it, or that it will keep going extremely long.

Further, the rich ought to be instructed not "to trust in unsure riches yet in the living God." One trap of abundance is the façade of security and joy it brings. Our jargon is brimming with words like "wellbeing net" and "savings" that give a false representation of dependence on cash to save us on troublesome occasions. However, Paul advises us that riches are "unsure" and are not deserving of our trust. Ask shrewd (and rich) Solomon. He will help you to remember the vacancy of riches: "He who loves silver won't be happy with silver." He will enlighten you concerning how momentary they are: "Riches surely make themselves wings; they fly away like a hawk toward paradise." Yet, the vast majority of all, he will help you to remember what we as a whole know: "As he came from his mom's belly, exposed will he return, to go as he came." When the securities exchange breakdowns, or the dollar jumps, or our country is crushed in war, how will you respond?

Does that change scare you? Trust "in the living God," and you will be fine through everything. Trust in riches, and you will be hopeless now and toward the end. Hardship to us if God should say, "Idiot! This night will expect your spirit of you; at that point whose will those things be which you have given".

However, how should rich individuals manage their cash? "Allow them to do good, that they are rich in good works, prepared to offer, willing to share, saving for themselves a good establishment for the future time, that they may lay hang on interminable life." There is a great idea to be done, and quite a bit of it very well may be finished with the abundance God has given us. Kindly see that this isn't good monetary arranging, actually talking. Spending our cash on helping other people and doing good isn't on the world's need list; however, it should be on our own. Christians in the main century "sold their assets and goods, and split them between all, as anybody had need." They worked, yet not to make sure they could have all that anyone could need for themselves: "Let him who took take no more, but instead let him work, working with his hands what is good, that he may have something to give him who has need." Listen further to John: "Yet whoever has this current world's goods, and sees his sibling out of luck, and quiets down his heart from him, how does the affection for God stay in him?". Being rich in good works isn't equivalent to considering good activities but neglecting to do them. It isn't accomplished by just focusing on individuals. Its achievement doesn't lay on wishing there was something we could do to help. In the most recent day, Jesus won't be intrigued by our bank articulation, however, by whether we utilized His things to help His kin. Do you breeze through that assessment?

It is the endowment of James, which reminds us what is valid pretty much the entirety of our precious belongings. Lectured with a similar fire-bellied conviction as the Old Testament prophets, James has cruel words for well-off individuals who abuse their riches. As per New Testament researcher Douglas Moo, James focuses on all affluent individuals, yet the individuals who put their abundance to profane closures. Or then again, the individuals who are just closefisted with it. For those devotees, James holds his harshest decisions.

Notwithstanding, James has a more widespread message as well. Regardless of whether we have riches or we don't, whether we abuse our money or we don't, our assets add up to practically nothing. Drawing on prior scriptural symbolism of moth and rust, James advises us that even our best natural belongings will one day be no more. Their Kingdom weight is slight. Their venture yields even less. Money and assets can't, and won't, give us what we need.

All in all, how would we get away?

To start with, feed on God, not things. Our quest for assets is a ton like attempting to fulfill a profound craving by eating a solitary lettuce leaf. It won't fill us. Our cravings must be fulfilled by the "bread of life," Jesus Christ, who guarantees, "Nobody who comes to me will at any point be ravenous, and nobody who trusts in me will at any point be parched once more."

Second, be liberal. Too often, we decide not to love our possessions too much, a well-intentioned mindset that is not accountable or discernible. The world will possibly realize we hold our assets freely if we hold them freely. It is the reason Jesus urges us to extremist demonstrations of liberality. Jesus orders this, not just because it's a "decent activity," but since it sets our hearts—and, subsequently, our feet—on an alternate way, away from the destruction James depicts.

These are realities we should talk over ourselves over and over. The radiance and sparkle of common goods are an incredible hallucination; however, the more we get back to these scriptural facts, the more they will begin to soak in.

SUMMARY

A clever closing idea would be that all choices of getting rich depend on accomplishing one or a few of the following realities:

1. **Be a producer** – Rather be a producer than a customer. Make an item or administration that individuals purchase like there's no tomorrow. Become a business visionary, online business visionary, or give significant abilities sought after and short supply.

2. **Follow the money** – Get drawn in with industry and establishment where the money is now in abundance (or will be soon). Huge organizations, beneficial organizations, the monetary or land area, or huge speculation projects.

3. **Become truly good with money** – Maximize your procuring potential, save like insane, contribute brilliantly or turn into a full-time financial backer all alone.

4. **Get enough consideration** – With enough consideration come promoters, and with publicists comes money. Be that as it may, acclaim is just for a small level of individuals; in any case, notoriety wouldn't be distinction any longer.

Turning out to be well off is normally a lifetime project that requires a ton of information, many brilliant key choices, a bunch of deliberately created abilities, ironclad self-administration, and some karma. Be that as it may, numerous people have shown it; it tends to be done.

Pick one of the ways, begin perusing histories of individuals who made abundance in your picked way, get instructed, and work keen and hard as damnation. What's more, above all, form the correct climate for yourself, since no one can succeed alone, we as whole need assistance.

Don't get fixated on money. Money certainly is significant; however, it's just one of the existing territories you need to deal with, and you would prefer not to relinquish your spirit by taking care of eagerness.

COPYRIGHT © 2021